I0560921

I Chose Me

From The Ashes of Narcissistic Love

Text copyright © 2025 Margarita M. Ortiz.

Illustration copyright © 2025 Margarita M. Ortiz.

All rights reserved.

Book designed by: Margarita M. Ortiz

No part of this book may be reproduced, distributed, or transmitted in any form or by any means, electronic or mechanical, including photocopying, recording, or by any information storage and retrieval system, electronic or mechanical methods, without written permission from the author, Except in the case of brief quotations embodied in reviews and certain other non-commercial uses permitted by copyright law.

To request permission, contact mslove.fwylh@gmail.com

Isbn: 978-1-967626-03-8 (Hard cover)
Isbn: 978-1-967626-02-1 (Softcover)

Author's Note

This book was written from the depths of my personal truth.
It holds pieces of my pain, my growth, my healing, and my voice
reclaimed.
While I stand firmly in my spiritual beliefs, I know that healing
takes many forms, and no one path looks the same.
So I offer these words with an open heart and open hands,
Not to instruct, but to invite.
Not to teach, but to walk beside you.
I wish to allow every reader to bring their own understanding of
grace, faith, or purpose to the table.

There is no right way to heal...only your way,
and I hope this meets you right where you are.

My writing style is intentionally sparse and emotionally
grounded, shaped by my desire to express the pivotal moments
in my life, those 'aha' moments, awakenings, and quiet
epiphanies, without dwelling in every painful detail.
I didn't write to spotlight my suffering or seek sympathy, but to
illuminate a path, however brief, that others might recognize as
their own.

It's not about retelling trauma, it's about resonance.
I wanted readers to feel seen, to connect through the spaces I
left open, spaces where they could insert their own memories,
feelings, and truths. This approach was inspired in part by
another writer whose work carries a similar emotional rhythm,
but leans more poetic. That influence helped me realize that
sometimes, less can say more. My goal was to create something
both personal and universal, a mirror, not just a memoir.

"You cannot pour from an empty cup."

This book is me filling mine... and maybe, just maybe, helping you fill yours too.

With every word, I offer you truth.
With every page, I offer you presence.
With this book, I offer you proof.
You are not alone.
You are not too far gone.
You are allowed to begin again.

Always,
Margarita M. Ortiz

About the Author

I am a mother of three. A survivor.
A woman who has walked through fire more than once, not because I wanted to, but because life gave me no other choice. From childhood to adulthood, I've carried the weight of emotional and physical trauma, life-altering, often invisible, sometimes paralyzing. I've known silence that screamed louder than words. I've known fear that curled itself around my bones. I've known what it means to be surrounded, and yet feel completely alone.
And still, I rose.
Not just once.
But over and over again.

I rescued myself when no one came. I peeled back the layers of pain, shame, and survival, and chose to face myself, fully, tenderly, honestly. I broke down the barriers that were meant to break me. I chose growth where there could've been bitterness.
I chose healing where there could've been hate.
I made the terrifying, holy decision to stop repeating what hurt me, and to begin something new. Not just for me, but for my children.

For the generations after me. For the little girl inside me who never stopped hoping.
This book was born out of that choice.
I wrote this because I know what it feels like to want love more than anything, and still feel starved of it. I know the ache of abandonment. The ache of being misunderstood. The ache of not even knowing yourself after surviving so much.
I know the sacred moment when you realize...
the love you've always needed starts with the love you give to yourself.

A Note Just for You

To the one holding this book,

If you made it this far, I already know something about you...
you are powerful.
Not because you were untouched, but because you were shaken,
stretched, and brought to your edge... and still, you came back
to yourself.
This book isn't just a collection of reflections, it's proof that
healing is real. That clarity is possible. That you are not alone.
If you're still in it, still navigating the fog, still questioning your
worth...I want you to hear this:
You are not crazy. You are not too much. You are not broken.
You are waking up.
You are remembering.
You are coming home to yourself.
Whether you're just beginning or years into your healing,
this is your reminder:
You are allowed to outgrow what once kept you safe. You are
allowed to change. You are allowed to be free.
You never needed permission to be whole.
But if you're looking for a sign...this is it.
I believe in your becoming.
I trust your story,
and I'm so proud of you for still being here.
Keep going.
Keep choosing you.
Again and again and again.

With love,
From one survivor to another

I Chose Me
From The Ashes of Narcissistic Love

Author & Illustrator: Margarita M. Ortiz

THE FOG OF IT ALL

The silent torment of emotional manipulation.

THE FOG OF IT ALL

"I kept calling it love, but it was me trying to
survive inside someone else's storm."

There were days I thought love was supposed
to feel like chaos. I thought the ache in my
chest was proof of how deep I could feel.
But all I was doing was holding my breath,
waiting for the storm to pass, calling the
lightning "intensity" and the silence "peace."

THE FOG OF IT ALL

"They convinced me I was hard to love,
just so I would never leave. But I did."

Their words were carefully woven nets, gentle
enough to sound like care, sharp enough to cut
my confidence. But something inside me
knew... and that knowing, even when it
whispered, became my way out.

THE FOG OF IT ALL

"I was loyal to a lie.
That truth broke my heart, but it also set me
free."

I grieved the illusion. I begged it to be real.
But when the lie crumbled, it left behind
something I hadn't seen in years: my own
reflection, steady, scarred, and still standing.

THE FOG OF IT ALL

"They weren't confused. They were controlling."

I used to explain their behavior away like it made it hurt less. Like if I could justify the pain, I wouldn't feel betrayed by it. But control doesn't look like confusion... it looks like someone who knows exactly how to keep you doubting yourself.

THE FOG OF IT ALL

"I was constantly walking on eggshells.
Now I dance freely on solid ground."

Back then, every word felt like a trap, every
silence a punishment. I didn't know love could
feel safe. But now my steps are my own, and
the ground doesn't crack beneath me anymore.

THE FOG OF IT ALL

"They kept moving the goalposts.
So I left the field."

I thought if I just tried harder, bent more, shrank
better, I'd finally win... but the rules kept
changing, and the game was rigged.
So I walked, and in walking, I won everything.

THE FOG OF IT ALL

"What I called 'love' was me trying to survive
emotional starvation."

I mistook breadcrumbs for devotion.
I convinced myself that their scraps meant
something sacred. Now I know... real love
doesn't leave you hungry.

THE FOG OF IT ALL

"I used to think I was overreacting.
Now I know I was under-protected."

They told me I was too sensitive, too emotional,
too much. But what I really was… was
unshielded. Alone, and learning now, that
sensitivity was a siren, warning me of danger I
wasn't allowed to name.

THE FOG OF IT ALL

"I didn't just leave them. I left the version of myself who thought pain was a fair price for love."

I loved, with open palms and aching ribs.
I stayed with hope and wounds both bleeding.
But I'm not that version of myself, anymore.
I found a different kind of love, the kind that doesn't hurt.

THE FOG OF IT ALL

"They didn't love me wrong.
They didn't love me at all."

That's the truth I kept running from. I tried to
patch it up with maybes and memories.
But now I let it sit in the light... and it doesn't
destroy me. It frees me.

THE FOG OF IT ALL

"I thought breaking up would end the abuse.
I didn't know it would take time to unlearn the
pain."

Leaving was just the beginning. The ghosts
stayed for a while, showing up in mirrors and
quiet moments. But day by day, I'm learning to
live without the echo of their voice in my head.

THE FOG OF IT ALL

"They called it love.
But love doesn't hurt like that."

Love doesn't twist. It doesn't leave bruises in places only I can feel. That wasn't love, and I don't have to call it that just because I wanted it to be.

THE FOG OF IT ALL

"They confused me so well, I forgot how to
trust myself.
I'm learning again."

Gaslight is a quiet war. I stopped knowing what
was real. But slowly, piece by piece, I'm coming
home to my intuition.
I'm still here. Still glowing.

THE FOG OF IT ALL

"The fear they planted in me doesn't run my life
anymore."

I used to flinch at kindness. I used to prepare
for rage like it was inevitable. But now?
I breathe. I stand still... and the fear doesn't get
to drive anymore.

THE FOG OF IT ALL

"There is no closure in pretending it wasn't
that bad."

I tried to wrap it up nicely. Tried to call it
complicated instead of cruel. But healing didn't
start until I said it out loud: it was abuse...
and that truth cracked the door wide open.

THE SHIFT BEGINS

The awakening. The gut whisper. The first cracks in the illusion.

THE SHIFT BEGINS

"I started noticing how I felt after being around
them... and it never felt good."

It didn't come like thunder. It came quietly, like
the ache after a bruise. Just a sinking feeling I
couldn't explain. But that feeling became my
compass.

THE SHIFT BEGINS

"I stopped explaining myself to someone who
never listened."

Every conversation felt like a maze built to trap
me. I talked in circles. I begged to be
understood. Then one day, I stopped.
In that silence, I heard myself for the first time.

THE SHIFT BEGINS

"One day, I stopped blaming myself, and everything started to change."

All the apologies I gave were to survive, not because I was wrong. The day I stopped taking responsibility for their cruelty was the day I remembered who I was.

THE SHIFT BEGINS

"It wasn't miscommunication. It was manipulation."

I kept thinking if I could just say it right, we'd finally be okay. But the message was never the problem... it was that they didn't care to hear it.

THE SHIFT BEGINS

"I used to ache for their presence. Now I crave their absence."

What I once called love, I now see as a trauma response. My body was always bracing.
I confused intensity with connection. But peace feels better.

THE SHIFT BEGINS

"The more I healed, the more I saw how much I had tolerated."

Healing didn't just bring clarity, it brought grief. Grief for how much I endured in the name of hope. But that grief was sacred. It told me the truth.

THE SHIFT BEGINS

"I no longer needed them to be the villain to
know I deserved better."

It wasn't about hate. It wasn't about revenge. It
was about knowing that I deserved something
softer, safer, truer. Even if they never admitted
what they did.

THE SHIFT BEGINS

"They used to make me feel crazy. Now I trust the voice that told me to run."

There was always a voice in me, whispering warnings I didn't want to hear. I hear it clearly now... and it's never been wrong.

THE SHIFT BEGINS

"I stopped calling it miscommunication when it was really emotional abuse."

The truth doesn't need to be dramatic to be devastating. It just needs to be spoken. Now that it's out loud, it's undeniable.

THE SHIFT BEGINS

"The day I chose truth over fantasy was the day
I finally breathed."

I didn't want to let go of what I thought we could
be. But the fantasy was feeding my silence.
The truth? The truth saved me.

THE SHIFT BEGINS

"I stopped fighting to be chosen and started choosing myself."

It wasn't a sudden moment. It was a slow shift. But one day, I saw the part of me begging for love... and I reached for it.

THE SHIFT BEGINS

"Their charm was the mask. The harm was the truth."

It's easy to miss the harm when it's wrapped in warmth. But once the mask slips, you can't unsee the damage. Now I choose truth, even when it hurts.

THE SHIFT BEGINS

"I realized I never felt safe with them. I just got used to the danger."

Comfort isn't always healthy. Sometimes it's just familiar. But real safety doesn't leave you shaking behind closed doors.

THE SHIFT BEGINS

"When I stopped trying to be perfect, I saw just
how impossible they made it."

No matter how good I was, it was never
enough. Not because I lacked, but because
their love was conditional. I'm done earning
love that should be freely given.

THE SHIFT BEGINS

"They never had to break me. They just kept me doubting myself long enough to do the job for them."

But that ends here. I see myself now... clearly, wholly, fiercely, and I will never doubt that voice again.

THE LEAVING

The decision. The breaking point. The first breath of freedom.

THE LEAVING

"I didn't leave because I stopped loving them. I left because I started loving myself."

That's what no one tells you...that sometimes walking away is the loudest kind of self-respect. I didn't want to go. I needed to, and that's a different kind of strength.

THE LEAVING

"One day I woke up and the fear of staying
finally outweighed the fear of leaving."

It wasn't a grand moment. No final blow. Just a
quiet knowing that this could not be the rest of
my life... and so I rose.

THE LEAVING

"I left with nothing but my truth... and that was enough."

No closure. No apology. No final conversation that made it make sense. Just me, and my knowing, and I carried that knowing like fire.

THE LEAVING

"I used to imagine leaving would destroy me.
Turns out, staying was what was killing me."

I thought I wouldn't survive the loss. But what I
lost in leaving was pain, and what I gained?
Everything I'd forgotten I deserved.

THE LEAVING

"I stopped waiting for them to become someone they never were."

They kept promising potential. But I lived with reality, and I chose to believe what I saw, not what I hoped.

THE LEAVING

"It wasn't just that I left. It was that I didn't go back."

Leaving is an act of courage. Not returning is an act of revolution.

THE LEAVING

"I left silently, but everything about me has been
louder since."

I didn't need to scream. I didn't need to explain.
My absence said it all.

THE LEAVING

"I thought I needed them to be okay.
Turns out, I just needed space to remember
who I was without them."

That space was scary at first... so quiet I could
hear every doubt echo. But then came the
clarity, and then came me.

THE LEAVING

"My leaving wasn't dramatic. It was sacred."

It wasn't about punishment. It wasn't revenge.
It was a quiet ceremony of reclaiming.
A holy exit.

THE LEAVING

"They called me selfish when I stopped
abandoning myself for them."

But I've learned: choosing myself isn't selfish.
It's survival, and now, it's also sacred.

THE LEAVING

"I didn't need them to hurt me again to know
they never stopped."

Even when it was quiet, it was still wrong. Even
when they weren't yelling, I was still hurting. I
don't need more proof. I need peace.

THE LEAVING

"I walked away from the illusion, not the love.
The love was never real."

That was the hardest part... admitting that what
I clung to was just a hope, not a home.
But truth tastes better than lies, even when it
burns going down.

THE LEAVING

"I stopped justifying my pain.
I started honoring it."

I don't owe anyone a reason for leaving.
My bruises were reason enough. Even the
ones you couldn't see.

THE LEAVING

"The version of me who stayed so long
deserved my compassion, not my shame."

Did the best possible, held on to beliefs, clung
to hope, gave love freely, and in the
end...walked away. That takes courage.
That's what makes a hero.

THE LEAVING

"I left for the part of me still waiting to be saved.
I came back instead."

No one showed up... so I did. And that part isn't
waiting anymore. Now it walks beside me.

NO CONTACT, FULL CLARITY

Silence as strength. Boundaries as healing. The voice returns.

NO CONTACT, FULL CLARITY

"No contact isn't cruelty. It's choosing peace over chaos."

They called it cold. They called it harsh. But they never called themselves out for the damage that made silence necessary.

NO CONTACT, FULL CLARITY

"I don't owe closure to the one who kept
wounding me."

Closure didn't come in a conversation. It came
in a decision: this ends here.

NO CONTACT, FULL CLARITY

"My peace became louder than their voice in
my head."

For a while, it echoed... what they said, what
they made me believe. But now? Now there's a
stillness in me where their chaos used to live.

NO CONTACT, FULL CLARITY

"They can't reach me anymore, not because I hate them, but because I love myself."

Boundaries aren't walls. They're doors that stay closed to what no longer belongs inside.

NO CONTACT, FULL CLARITY

"The silence between us is not empty. It's filled
with everything I reclaimed."

My breath. My time. My self-worth. Every inch
of quiet is a space I once gave away...and have
now returned to.

NO CONTACT, FULL CLARITY

"I stopped checking if they watched my stories.
I started writing my own."

I used to seek their shadow in everything.
Now, I turn toward the light and walk forward.

NO CONTACT, FULL CLARITY

"I didn't block them out of spite. I blocked them
out of survival."

I didn't need one more excuse. One more guilt
trip. One more spiral. I needed space. Real
space... and I gave it to myself.

NO CONTACT, FULL CLARITY

"I used to wonder what they'd think of my healing. Now I don't care."

This journey is mine. They don't get to be the center of a story they tried to ruin.

NO CONTACT, FULL CLARITY

"They lost access to me the moment I realized I
never truly had them."

All those conversations, all that pleading...
it was me trying to connect with someone who
wasn't even showing up. But I'm here now.
For me.

NO CONTACT, FULL CLARITY

"No contact didn't erase the pain. It just stopped the bleeding."

Healing still hurts. But at least now, the wound isn't being reopened every time I try to breathe.

NO CONTACT, FULL CLARITY

"The urge to reach out was strong.
The urge to heal was stronger."

I wrote the texts. I deleted them. I screamed
into pillows. I cried in silence... and I didn't go
back.

NO CONTACT, FULL CLARITY

"Every day I don't break no contact is a day I
choose myself."

Some days, that choice is hard. But I never
regret it. Not once.

NO CONTACT, FULL CLARITY

"They wanted access to the healed me without being held accountable for how they broke me."

But healing doesn't mean forgetting... and forgiveness doesn't mean returning.

NO CONTACT, FULL CLARITY

"Their silence after I left was the final
confirmation I needed."

They didn't chase me. They didn't fight for me.
In that quiet, I heard the truth louder than ever:
it was never love.

NO CONTACT, FULL CLARITY

"I kept thinking I'd feel free after I cut them off.
What I felt first was grief, and then, finally...
relief."

It's not linear. It's messy. But it's real, and I
wouldn't trade this kind of peace for anything.

REBUILDING ME

The return to self. The reckoning. The rise.

REBUILDING ME

"I started with the smallest things... drinking water, resting, being kind to myself.
That was the revolution."

Healing didn't look like a big moment. It looked like making tea without panic. Sleeping through the night. Saying, you're okay now, and meaning it.

REBUILDING ME

"I no longer asked, 'Why did they treat me like that?' I asked, 'Why did I stay?' Then I answered with compassion, not shame."

The staying wasn't weakness. It was hope, trauma, confusion. I don't blame myself anymore. I honor myself for surviving.

REBUILDING ME

"My voice came back first as a whisper.
Now it's thunder."

At first, I only said it to myself: I didn't deserve
that. Now I say it out loud. In rooms. In writing.
In the way I carry myself.

REBUILDING ME

"Loving myself felt foreign at first... like trying on clothes that didn't fit yet. But they were mine."

It wasn't instant. I had to grow into it. I had to teach myself how to receive my own tenderness. But now? I wear self-love like skin.

REBUILDING ME

"I stopped calling myself broken. I started calling myself rebuilding."

There is no shame in starting over. I'm not a ruin... I'm a work in progress. This version of me is my favorite yet.

REBUILDING ME

"Peace felt uncomfortable at first. I wasn't used
to love without tension."

I didn't know what it was like to rest and not
fear the aftermath. But slowly, peace became
my baseline... not a rare reward.

REBUILDING ME

"Every time I chose rest over hustle, silence over proving, I healed the part of me they tried to erase."

My worth was never in how much I gave. It was always in who I am when I stop performing.

REBUILDING ME

"I used to flinch when someone was kind to me.
Now I soften."

Kindness used to confuse me. Now I let it in.
Not because I need it...
but because I deserve it.

REBUILDING ME

"The best apology is how I love myself now."

I spent years waiting for an apology that never came. So I gave one to myself... and then lived like I meant it.

REBUILDING ME

"I used to miss who I was before the abuse. Now I love who I became because of what I survived."

There's power in the aftermath. I didn't just survive. I transformed.

REBUILDING ME

"Healing didn't make me unbreakable. It made me whole."

I'm not trying to be untouchable. I just don't bleed for people who wouldn't bandage me anymore.

REBUILDING ME

"I didn't find myself again. I built myself from the ground up."

Piece by piece. Day by day. With gentleness and fire. This version of me is not a return... it's a rebirth.

REBUILDING ME

"Now when my body tightens, I listen.
It's not overreacting... it's remembering."

My nervous system isn't broken. It's a survivor,
too. I hold and thank it now. We're learning
safety together.

REBUILDING ME

"I no longer wait to be loved right. I start by loving me fully."

What I expected from them, I now give to myself... presence, patience, protection, and it's enough.

REBUILDING ME

"My boundaries now feel like love songs to
myself."

Every 'no' is a poem. Every silence, a prayer.
Every closed door, a sanctuary I built with my
own hands.

LOVING AGAIN
(WITHOUT LOOSING MYSELF)

Softness with boundaries. Love without surrender.
Choosing with eyes open.

LOVING AGAIN
(WITHOUT LOOSING MYSELF)

"This time, I bring all of me into love, and I watch who can hold it without asking me to shrink."

I am no longer available for half-love. For conditional care. For becoming small so someone else can feel big.

LOVING AGAIN
(WITHOUT LOOSING MYSELF)

"Before, I waited to be chosen. Now, I choose."

I used to wonder if I was enough.
Now I ask if they are.
I don't chase love... I discern it.

LOVING AGAIN
(WITHOUT LOOSING MYSELF)

"Loving again felt terrifying, until I realized love isn't the threat. Losing myself is."

So I stay rooted in me. I don't disappear into someone else anymore. I bring my full self, and I stay home within it.

LOVING AGAIN
(WITHOUT LOOSING MYSELF)

"I don't ignore red flags anymore, not even the
pink ones."

The first sign is enough now. I don't need
evidence in blood to trust my gut.

LOVING AGAIN
(WITHOUT LOOSING MYSELF)

"Now, when something feels off, I don't explain
it away. I walk away."

My intuition doesn't need to submit a report.
It's whispers are reason enough.

LOVING AGAIN
(WITHOUT LOOSING MYSELF)

"I no longer mistake anxiety for attraction."

That rush, that spark... it used to feel like love.
It was survival. Trauma. Confusion. Real love
feels calm. It breathes.

LOVING AGAIN
(WITHOUT LOOSING MYSELF)

"I don't need chaos to feel alive anymore."

Love, to me now, is a warm room I don't have to
earn my place in. It doesn't come with dread.
It comes with ease.

LOVING AGAIN
(WITHOUT LOOSING MYSELF)

"This time, I move slower. Not from fear, but
from wisdom."

There's no rush. Love that's meant for me will
wait, grow, unfold. I don't perform. I observe.

LOVING AGAIN
(WITHOUT LOOSING MYSELF)

"I check in with myself more than I check their texts."

The most important relationship I have is the one between me and my nervous system.
If it's not calm, I listen.

LOVING AGAIN
(WITHOUT LOOSING MYSELF)

"If I have to abandon myself to keep someone,
they're not mine to keep."

That's non-negotiable now. I can love deeply
without self-erasing.

LOVING AGAIN
(WITHOUT LOOSING MYSELF)

"I don't compromise on peace anymore."

If it costs me my mental health, my clarity, my
sense of self... it's too expensive.

LOVING AGAIN
(WITHOUT LOOSING MYSELF)

"My love is sacred. Not everyone gets access."

Not out of bitterness, but out of self-honoring.
I used to hand my heart to those who hadn't
earned it. Now I require capacity, not charm.

LOVING AGAIN
(WITHOUT LOOSING MYSELF)

"I'm not afraid to walk away, even from
someone I love."

Because love isn't enough. Safety. Respect.
Reciprocity. That's the standard now.

LOVING AGAIN
(WITHOUT LOOSING MYSELF)

"Loving again doesn't mean forgetting what I
survived. It means loving from the wholeness
that survival created."

I'm not naïve. I'm not hard. I'm awake...
and from here, love gets to be real.

LOVING AGAIN
(WITHOUT LOOSING MYSELF)

"Now, I'm the home I return to... even when I'm
with someone else."

Love isn't losing myself in another. It's meeting
them, while staying rooted in me.

THE NEW STANDARD

Peace. Power. Presence... and nothing less.

THE NEW STANDARD

"I no longer feel guilty for choosing peace. I feel grounded."

Before, calm felt like emptiness. Now it feels like everything I fought for.

THE NEW STANDARD

"I used to be addicted to fixing. Now I'm devoted to protecting my peace."

Not everyone gets access. Not every story needs saving. I am not a rehab center for broken behavior.

THE NEW STANDARD

"If it costs me my voice, it's too expensive."

That includes relationships, opportunities, and
old identities. Silence was once survival...
now, it's a choice, not a cage.

THE NEW STANDARD

"I walk away faster now, and I don't explain why."

I used to narrate my pain to be believed. Now, I believe myself, and that's enough.

THE NEW STANDARD

"Healing didn't just give me peace. It gave me standards."

I don't settle for almost-love, bare-minimum respect, or people who only show up when I shrink. That version of me is gone.

THE NEW STANDARD

"They don't get to decide who I am anymore.
I do."

For so long I was shaped by what they said I
was. Now, I'm defined by what I know I am.
Free. Whole. Worthy.

THE NEW STANDARD

"I used to fear being too much. Now I fear going back to too little."

I will never shrink again to be loved. If I'm too much, they're not enough.

THE NEW STANDARD

"My softness is not a weakness. It's my power
wrapped in gentleness."

I've learned to hold both strength and
tenderness. I don't harden to protect...
I expand to heal.

THE NEW STANDARD

"I don't just survive now.
I live."

I laugh louder. I rest without guilt. I take up space. I let myself want more... and I let myself have it.

THE NEW STANDARD

"I am no longer defined by what I endured.
I am shaped by what I chose after."

What they did matters. But who I became in the
aftermath? That's my legacy.

THE NEW STANDARD

"I wake up in a life that feels like mine now."

Not built on their expectations. Not filtered through fear. This life? This body? This path? It's mine.

THE NEW STANDARD

"My nervous system is learning safety...
and that's a miracle."

Every calm breath is proof that I made it.
That I rewrote what love and life mean for me.

THE NEW STANDARD

"I hold space for joy now, without waiting for it to be taken."

I used to brace for impact. Now I open my palms, and I let good things stay.

THE NEW STANDARD

""I trust myself more than anyone's opinion."

Even when I'm unsure. Even when I stumble.
My inner voice is the authority now.

THE NEW STANDARD

"I'm not healed because I never get triggered. I'm healed because I no longer betray myself when I do."

Triggers come. But I meet them with gentleness, not shame. I meet me there, every time.

THE NEW STANDARD

"I am not afraid to take up space anymore."

In rooms. In conversations. In this world.
I belong everywhere I bring my wholeness.

TO THE ONE WHO'S STILL THERE

A letter to the version of me still in the fire.

TO THE ONE WHO'S STILL THERE

"I see you. I remember what it felt like to forget who you were."

That disorienting fog. The way your heart clenches at every tone shift. The constant second-guessing. I lived there too. I want you to know: You are not crazy. You are not too sensitive. You are being harmed... and none of this is your fault.

TO THE ONE WHO'S STILL THERE

"I know you're tired. I know you're scared,
and I know you think leaving will break you.
But staying is what's breaking you."

This isn't what love feels like. Real love doesn't
feel like begging. Like silence. Like walking on
shattered eggshells.

TO THE ONE WHO'S STILL THERE

"You don't have to prove you're good enough to be loved. You already are."

They won't see it. That doesn't mean it's not there. Their inability to love you fully is not a reflection of your worth...
it's a reflection of their limitations.

TO THE ONE WHO'S STILL THERE

"You are not the problem."

I know how many times they've made you feel like you are. How often they twist your words, your reactions, your pain into weapons against you. But listen to me: the way they treat you is not your responsibility to fix.

TO THE ONE WHO'S STILL THERE

"It's okay if you're not ready to leave yet.
Just promise me this: you'll keep listening to
that quiet voice inside."

The one that whispers, this isn't love.
That voice is not weakness... it's wisdom.
It's the first piece of you coming back.

TO THE ONE WHO'S STILL THERE

"You don't have to wait until it gets worse to say it's enough."

You don't need another scar to justify leaving. Your pain is already valid. Your knowing is already enough.

TO THE ONE WHO'S STILL THERE

"I know you miss the good moments.
That's how they keep you."

But the good times don't erase the harm. They make the harm more confusing. It's okay to grieve what you thought it could be, even while you admit what it really is.

TO THE ONE WHO'S STILL THERE

"You don't need anyone to believe you but yourself."

The gaslighting, the subtle digs, the public charm that hides private cruelty, it makes you doubt your reality. But I believe you. I trust your truth. Keep going.

TO THE ONE WHO'S STILL THERE

"You're not weak for staying. You're surviving."

But survival is not the same as living...
and you deserve more than just making it
through.

TO THE ONE WHO'S STILL THERE

"There will be a day when your name doesn't tremble in your own mouth."

A day when you won't flinch at kindness. When you won't question your worth. When your voice will come back like a storm... and you'll be the one holding the sky.

TO THE ONE WHO'S STILL THERE

"You are allowed to want more."

More peace. More ease. More mornings that don't start with dread. More love that doesn't come with bruises... emotional or otherwise.

TO THE ONE WHO'S STILL THERE

"This pain won't last forever. But your courage?
That will."

You're already brave. Not because you're not
afraid, but because you're still here.

TO THE ONE WHO'S STILL THERE

"One day, you'll look back and see this moment
not as the end, but as the beginning of
everything."

The first crack in the armor. The first whisper of
truth. The first time you said, I deserve more,
even if only in your heart.
That's the beginning. That's your becoming.

TO THE ONE WHO'S STILL THERE

I promise... there is life after this, and it's so
much bigger than what they tried to contain you
in.
I'm living it now, and I'll be here, holding the
light, until you find your way out.

THE LETTERS I NEVER SENT

What I couldn't say then. What I now say for me.

THE LETTERS I NEVER SENT

To the One Who Hurt Me,

You confused control with love. You made me
doubt myself, unravel myself, shrink myself...
just to make you feel bigger. I bent until I almost
disappeared, and still, you wanted more.
But I've stopped trying to be enough for
someone who can't even be honest with
themselves.
You don't get to have me anymore.
Not my body. Not my mind. Not my spirit...
and definitely not my silence.

THE LETTERS I NEVER SENT

To My Past Self,

I forgive you.
For staying too long. For loving too hard. For
trying too much. You weren't weak, you were
loyal. Hopeful. Human.
You did what you had to do to survive, and look
at you now... still standing. Still soft. Still
reaching for healing.
You didn't fail. You endured. Now, you rise.

THE LETTERS I NEVER SENT

To the Narcissist,

You were the storm. I was the shelter.
But you convinced me I was the damage.
I've spent enough time rebuilding what you tried
to tear down.
You taught me everything I never want again...
and for that, strangely, I thank you.
Not because it was worth it. But because I was.

THE LETTERS I NEVER SENT

To the Love I Deserved,

I used to dream of you with desperation in my
bones. I thought if I could just be better, you'd
arrive.
But now I know: you're not a fantasy.
You're the way I treat myself. The way I rest.
The way I refuse to settle.
You are real.
I'm not waiting anymore. I'm becoming the
space where you'll feel at home.

THE LETTERS I NEVER SENT

To My Future,

I'm not afraid of you anymore.
I used to dread what was next, because I didn't
believe I could live without them.
But I can. I do. I will.
You are wide open, full of light, and finally...
mine.

THE LETTERS I NEVER SENT

To the Apology That Never Came,

I don't need you to say you're sorry.
I used to ache for it. Rehearse it in my mind.
But I know what you did.
I know what I felt and I don't need your
validation to name it.
I free myself... without your permission.

THE LETTERS I NEVER SENT

To My Anger,

I welcome you.
You're not ugly. You're sacred.
You showed up when I was too hurt to speak.
Too confused to act.
You kept me alive in your fire.
Now I let you speak, and then I let you rest.

THE LETTERS I NEVER SENT

To My Peace,

You are not boring.
You are not weakness.
You are the loudest reclamation I've ever made.
Every day I choose you, I undo years of chaos.
You are home... and I'm staying.

RECLAMATION

The life I'm building now. The self I finally recognize.
The freedom I fought for.

RECLAMATION

"This time, I don't just want peace. I want joy.
Loud, untamed, belly-laughing joy."

For too long, I only aimed for 'not hurting.' But I
deserve delight. Spontaneity. Mornings that feel
like music. I give myself permission to enjoy
being alive.

RECLAMATION

"I no longer edit myself to be palatable. If I'm
too much, they can go hungry."

I used to shrink my voice, my needs, my light.
Now I show up fully. Unapologetically.
I didn't survive all that to live quietly.

RECLAMATION

"I'm no longer proving I'm good enough.
I'm simply being, and that is enough."

I don't hustle for love. I don't beg for belonging.
I am the belonging.

RECLAMATION

"I didn't just reclaim my life... I redesigned it."

New routines. New friendships. New dreams.
I no longer build around other people's comfort.
I build around my own truth.

RECLAMATION

"I laugh now without checking if it's too loud."

That might seem small, but to me, it's everything. I used to silence myself to stay safe. Now, I celebrate my sound.

RECLAMATION

"I wear clothes I like. I decorate my space how I want. I move how I feel. Everything is mine now."

Even the smallest choices feel like freedom. Because they are.

RECLAMATION

"I no longer wait for someone to invite me to the table. I build my own, and fill it with love."

Real love. Safe people. Whole food. Loud music. Big dreams. Laughter that lingers.

RECLAMATION

"My body is no longer a battleground. It is a
sanctuary."

I thank it. I feed it. I rest it. I dress it in softness
and strength. I don't punish it anymore for what
others did.

RECLAMATION

"I take up space like I was meant to."

I speak clearly. I show up fully. I let people feel the weight of my presence. I don't apologize for existing.

RECLAMATION

"I trust my joy now. I don't question when it arrives. I welcome it in like an old friend."

Because joy isn't a trick. It's not a trap. It's a signpost: you made it.

RECLAMATION

"I say yes to things I love, and no without explanation."

I don't over-explain. I don't convince. My boundaries are sacred, not optional.

RECLAMATION

"My life doesn't revolve around what I survived.
It revolves around what I'm creating."

Yes, it shaped me. But it doesn't define me.
I do.

RECLAMATION

"I am no longer surviving their damage. I am living my design."

It's beautiful here. Messy. True. Real. Mine.

RECLAMATION

"I am proud of me. I say it out loud. Often."

Not because I need approval, but because I finally believe it, and it deserves to be celebrated.

RECLAMATION

"I didn't just get my life back. I made a new one."

It's not built from fear. It's built from fire, softness, clarity, and choice.... and every day, it gets better.

A LOVE LETTER TO MY OWN BECOMING

I didn't find myself. I came back for me.

A LOVE LETTER TO MY OWN BECOMING

"Dear me,
You stayed.
When it would've been easier to disappear,
to shut down, to give in... you stayed.
In rooms that dimmed you.
In silence that hurt you.
In love that starved you.
You stayed with you...
and for that, I love you."

A LOVE LETTER TO MY OWN BECOMING

"You walked through fire and carried your own
ashes."
There were days you forgot your name. Forgot
your light. Forgot your worth.
But you never fully gave up.
You whispered your truth into the dark... and
even when no one answered, you listened.

A LOVE LETTER TO MY OWN BECOMING

"You stopped asking others to choose you, and
chose yourself instead."
That was the moment everything changed.
Not when they apologized. Not when they left.
Not when the pain stopped.
But when you said,
"No more."
"No more hiding. No more shrinking. No more
waiting to be saved."
That was the beginning of everything.

A LOVE LETTER TO MY OWN BECOMING

"I love how you came back different...
but still you."
Wiser. Softer. Stronger.
You didn't harden, you deepened.
You didn't close, you clarified.
And now? You shine.
But not for them.
For you.

A LOVE LETTER TO MY OWN BECOMING

"This love letter isn't about perfection.
It's about presence."
I see you now. In every mirror. Every breath.
Every moment you choose peace instead of
panic, truth instead of silence, you instead of
them.

A LOVE LETTER TO MY OWN BECOMING

"I love the way you protect your softness now."
You don't let anyone near your heart who hasn't
earned it, and still, you stay open.
That's the bravest thing of all.

A LOVE LETTER TO MY OWN BECOMING

"I love how you celebrate now."
The tiny wins. The quiet mornings. The deep
belly laughs.
You're not just surviving... you're living,
and you don't wait for someone to clap for you.
You dance in your own joy.

A LOVE LETTER TO MY OWN BECOMING

"Thank you for not giving up on me."
I was waiting here the whole time.
In the freedom. In the stillness.
In the life that finally feels like home.

A LOVE LETTER TO MY OWN BECOMING

Signed with the deepest love,
Me.

Even from the ashes of our deepest wounds, something beautiful can rise,
when we choose to become the flame reborn,
not just the remnants of the fire.

May these words find you where you are and honor the truth of your journey.

If these words found a home in your heart, and you know someone whose days feel a little darker, consider passing along this book, or gifting them their own special copy.

Let it carry the warmth of your heart, a quiet reminder that they are not alone, they are deeply loved, and that hope still lingers in every turned page.

Acknowledgments

To my children,

Thank you for giving me purpose when I felt lost, for loving me without question, and for being the greatest reasons I chose healing over hiding. You are my heart in human form, and every step I take forward is for you.

To every survivor, who has lived in silence, shame, or fear,

Thank you for existing, for enduring, and for reminding the world what true strength looks like. This book was written with you in mind. You are seen here. You are safe here.

To the ancestors who came before me,

I honor both the pain you carried and the paths you never had the chance to walk. I break the patterns not in anger, but in love. I walk a new road so that my children, and their children, will walk freer.

To those who caused me pain,

I acknowledge you, not to excuse the harm, but to mark the moment I stopped carrying it.
Your actions shaped parts of me, but they do not define me.
You taught me what I will never again accept... and for that, I found my boundaries, my voice, my worth.
I release you, not for you, but for me.
Because I choose peace. I choose healing. I choose freedom.

Acknowledgments

To the version of me that didn't give up,

Thank you for surviving, for holding on, for whispering "keep going" in the dark. You are the reason this book exists. You are the beginning of every page.

To all the blessings I have received, both big and small, loud and quiet,

Thank you for reminding me that even in the storm, there is beauty.
Even in the breaking, there is becoming.
Even in the silence, there is guidance.

To this very moment,

I honor you. This now, this breath, this chapter of becoming, it is sacred. It is proof that healing is happening.
That I made it.
That I am still here.

Dedication

For the woman I used to be,
The one who endured the unspoken,
carried the unbearable,
and still found the strength to keep breathing.

For the girl inside me,
who never stopped hoping, even in the silence.
You made it. I see you now.

For my children,
the reason I chose to break the cycle instead of continuing
it.
You are the light I never knew I was walking toward.
This healing is my gift to you.

And for every soul who has ever felt unloved, unseen, or
unheard,
You are not alone.
This book is your mirror.
Your permission.
You are worthy of a life that feels like peace.

www.ingramcontent.com/pod-product-compliance
Lightning Source LLC
Chambersburg PA
CBHW031525120626
46545CB00005B/1999